LIFE STORY
&
LEAVE A LEGACY
JOURNAL

Melanie Johnson
& Jenn Foster

©2016 Elite Online Publishing
63 East 11400 South Suite #230
Sandy, UT 84070
info@bookwritingretreats.com

ISBN-13: 978-1530571116

ISBN-10: 1530571111

Introduction

Welcome to your journal to record memories and thoughts about your childhood years, teen years, young adulthood, and later years to help track your life story and leave a legacy. This journal is a place to preserve memories and discovers hidden aspects of yourself and your journey that will encourage and inspire others with your stories. This journal was created to work in tandem with the workbook ***How to Write Your Life Story and Leave a Legacy:*** *A Story Starter Guide & Workbook to Write your Autobiography and Memoir.*

By Jenn Foster and Melanie Johnson

Available on Amazon: http://amzn.to/1U384yf

"Every day of your life is a day of history." - Arabic proverb

DATE:_____

DATE:_____

DATE:_____

DATE:_____

DATE:_____

DATE:_____

DATE:_____

DATE:_____

DATE:_____

DATE:_____

DATE:_____

Elite Online Publishing is The Brand Building Publisher. We help busy entrepreneurs, business leaders, and professional athletes Create, Publish, and Market their book, to build their business and brand. We are passionate about Authors sharing their stories, knowledge and expertise to help others.

www.EliteOnlinePublishing.com

Made in the USA
San Bernardino, CA
30 March 2019